Permission to Mourn

A New Way to Do Grief

TOM ZUBA

Bish Press

www.TomZuba.com
Rockford, IL USA

Permission to Mourn:
A New Way to Do Grief
by Tom Zuba

Second Printing – February 2015
ISBN: 978-1-60047-565-8
Library of Congress Control Number: 2014956218

Printed in the U.S.A.

0   1   2   3   4   5   6   7   8   9   10   11

To my son Sean
my greatest teacher
my fellow traveler in this earth school
and a most fascinating
wise old soul.
Thank you for choosing me to be your dad.
I love you dearly.
Now and forever.

FOREWORD

by Gary Zukav

Author of *The Seat of the Soul and Spiritual Partnership*

I recommend with joy Tom Zuba's exquisite, perceptive, and profound celebration of life, *Permission to Mourn*. Despite its title, it is actually a book about permission to live. It takes us where we all now need to go and gently, kindly shows us a path. For me, that is the path to Authentic Power – fulfillment, meaning, and joy – a life filled with love, a life without fear, vital, creative, and caring. In my experience, this life does not come easily, but recognizing the possibility of it, holding strongly the intention to create it, and using your every experience – including grief and loss – to guide you towards it, leads to an entirely new human experience. After a while, perhaps a long while, and perhaps even after the fact, you recognize in your own way that an ignition has occurred within you, lift-off has happened, and you are heading towards – or entering – uncharted realms of meaning, fulfillment, and power. Your work is not done at this stage, but you are on your way. A new life is coming into being in you, choice by choice, and you are flying.

A species-wide transformation of consciousness is expanding human experience beyond the limitations of the five senses. We are becoming multisensory. Nonphysical dynamics beneath appearances are becoming visible and our roles in them, too. This has never happened to our entire species, and now it is happening within a few generations. From the perspective of our evolution, a few generations are less than a heartbeat, less than an eye blink, less than a nanosecond. We sense ourselves as immortal souls and mortal personalities at the same time. We see the world as meaningful instead of random. We discover opportunities to grow spiritually wherever we look. At first we long to believe that the Universe is alive, wise, and compassionate. Then we begin to believe that it is.

Then we experience that it is. The path that Tom Zuba describes in *Permission to Mourn* takes us there.

A new understanding of power as the alignment of the personality with the soul is replacing the old understanding of power as the ability to manipulate and control. Creating the new power requires emotional awareness — never suppressing, repressing, or denying an emotion. It requires choices that create consequences for which you are willing to assume responsibility. It demands commitment, courage, compassion, and consciousness communications and actions. This is the hard work that Tom Zuba reminds us so gently and often is necessary. We must choose, moment to moment, between love and fear. The choice to believe that you are alone, invisible, and powerless, in this case that someone you loved dearly has been tragically taken, is a choice of fear. The choice to believe that the soul of the one you dearly love has returned home to nonphysical reality in a manner, place, and time of its choosing and yet remains with you, is the choice of love. The new way to grieve requires choosing love.

Emotional awareness, intention, choice, and responsibility are the tools of creating authentic power. They are also the new way to do grief. We will all create authentic power sooner or later. It is now required for human evolution. Be gentle with yourself. You are not judged when you choose fear. You suffer the painful consequences of your choice. You are not judged when you choose love. You bloom in the blissful consequences of your choice. *Permission to Mourn* is about becoming aware, experiencing the enormity, power, and grace of your life, and creating with love each moment. This is what we were born to do.

Love,
Gary Zukav

TABLE OF CONTENTS

INTRODUCTION

I am an ordinary person. I'm just like you. As I reflect back, I realize I've lived through extraordinary circumstances, and made different choices. Not at first. At first I made the same choices most of us make. We make them consciously and subconsciously. When I noticed, however, that the choices I was making were creating pain on top of pain on top of unbearable pain, I decided to make different choices. And I did. Over and over and over again. You can, too. Along the way, I discovered a new way to do grief. That's why I wrote this book. To share with you all I've learned.

Shortly after our 18-month-old daughter Erin, our first-born, died suddenly in 1990, my wife Trici (pronounced Trish) and I returned to work at our downtown Chicago jobs; Trici to the American Cancer Society and me to the national office of Easter Seals. We didn't know any better. How could we?

As often as possible, in those tentative, fragile, first weeks, I'd leave work promptly at 5:00pm. From Lake Street, I'd walk south on Michigan Avenue until I arrived at Trici's building. Together we'd walk to the Lake Street train and make our way home to our suburban Oak Park apartment, still quiet beyond belief, and empty. So very empty. One day sticks in my mind like a Polaroid picture. Trici's colleague, our friend Sherry, pressed the down button and waited at the elevator with us. With soft, tender love Sherry smiled gently and said, "My prayer is that the rest of your life will be uneventful and boring." I knew what she meant.

My life has been anything but.

Nine years later, the inexplicable, unimaginable explosiveness of Trici's sudden death on New Year's Day 1999 was not lost on me. I had two prayers. I did not want to waste this experience and I wanted to be surrounded by people much wiser than me.

I haven't and I most certainly was.

Less than four months after Trici's death I was telling our story to millions of people on The Oprah Winfrey Show with Gary Zukav, NYTimes best-selling author of *The Seat of the Soul.* As I said that day to Oprah and Gary, "I'm not at all surprised to be here. I'm surprised I'm here as quickly as I am."

In the 15 years since Trici's death I have marinated in the teachings and wisdom of a handful of ordinary people, who by the choices they've made have lived extraordinary lives. Many of these people were "introduced" to me, and perhaps to you, by Oprah Winfrey on her television show. Their wisdom is woven throughout these pages and in everything I am and do.

My great teachers include:

Debbie Ford, author of *The Dark Side of the Light Chasers.* "You must go into the dark in order to bring forth your light. When we suppress any feeling or impulse, we are also suppressing its polar opposite."

Byron Katie, author of *Loving What Is.* "Everything happens for me, not to me" and "Just keep coming home to yourself. You are the one you've been waiting for."

Don Miguel Ruiz, author of *The Four Agreements.* "The first agreement is to *be impeccable with your word* ... The word is not just a sound or written symbol. The word is a force; it is the power you have to express and communicate, to think, and thereby create the events of your life." "The second agreement is *don't take anything personally*."

Colin Tipping, author of *Radical Forgiveness.* "It is only when we give ourselves permission to access our pain that our healing begins. The healing journey is essentially an emotional one."

Eckhart Tolle, author of *The Power of Now.* "The fact is that you are resisting what is. You are making the present moment into an enemy."

Iyanla Vanzant, author of *Yesterday, I Cried.* In the fall of 1998, while sitting in a hotel room in Washington, DC with the television on, I heard Iyanla say to Oprah, "Remind yourself over and over that, 'I am the beloved. I am the beloved.'" I wrote those four words down on the hotel stationery and have never been the same.

John E. Welshons, author of *Awakening From Grief: Finding The Way Back To Joy.* "We are not our bodies, and our relationships don't exist in our bodies - they exist in our hearts, in our mind, in our soul."

Gary Zukav, author of *The Seat of the Soul.* "Eventually, you will come to understand that love heals everything, and love is all there is."

I am grateful to each of these bright lights for the work they have done and the gifts they have given. To me. To the world.

When my 13-year-old son Rory died from brain cancer on February 22, 2005 I knew I could heal. I had done it before. I wasn't sure,

 3

however, if I had the energy and determination to do the work. Not again. Healing from the death of someone you love dearly is such hard, hard work. When Erin died, I didn't believe there was a light at the end of the tunnel. Not this tunnel. Only to find out, that yes, indeed, there was a light. When Trici died nine years later, knowing that the light at tunnel's end existed colored that journey for me. And when Rory died, not only was I certain there was light at the end of the tunnel, but, this time, the tunnel itself was lit. And that made all the difference. That knowing allowed me to become the observer and active participant in my own healing.

This is the book I wish I had read after Erin died, and after Trici died, and after Rory died. But I wasn't ready. Not then. First, I had to live it. So I could write it. For you. But you are ready, or you wouldn't be reading these words. You are ready to do grief a new way.

My new prayer is that you will set the intention to see with new eyes, to hear with new ears and to feel with a new heart. That you will pay more attention to your heart and less attention to your head as you read my words. That you will allow yourself to feel. All of it. Throughout these pages, I offer you hope and possibility. While the darkness has purpose, it is not meant to be your forever place. There is a new way to do grief. A way rooted in hope, and possibility with the promise of a new, joy-filled life. Say yes. Say yes. Say yes. To life. To love. To you.

If not now, when?

1. We Dance Between Both Worlds

The death of someone we love
dearly
cracks us open.
Big time.
It's supposed to.

It did me.

And for a time —
which varies from person-to-person
and can be a few days
or a week or two
or a month
or many months
or a year
or years
or the rest of our life —
some (many)
will dance between both worlds.

I do.

Do you?
Did you?
Are you still?
Dancing?

We dance between this world
and the next
when our beloved dies.
When she takes her last breath.
When he leaves his body.

We leave.
Too.
This physical plane.
For a time.
To be with them.
Where they are now.

And the dance begins.
Between both worlds.
Where all things are possible.

It's during this time that it's helpful
and healing
and so often frightening
to question everything.

Everything.

Because it's all been cracked.
Open.

It no longer matters (really)
what your parents
your family
your teachers
your priests and ministers

and friends
believe.
What matters now is what you believe.

Because when someone you love
dearly
dies
you don't know.
What you believe.
Anymore.
Not really.

About life
and love
and meaning
and purpose
and why-was-I-born
and why-did-she-die
and could-I-have-saved-him?

And death.

You don't really know what you believe about death anymore.
Because someone you love so much has gone and done it.
Died.
So you question everything you once held true
about death.
You question all the beliefs you've clung to
without ever having to really think about them.
To examine them.
To question them.
Until now.

You simply inhaled what was passed on to you.
Like the rest of us.

But not anymore.
You just can't.

So you question.
Everything.
As I said
you're supposed to.

Is there a God?
If there is
what is he/she/it/they?
And if there is a God
what did he/she/it/they have to do with the death
of this person I love?
So much.
And do we still exist after we die?
In some form or another?
And is there a heaven?
If there is
what is it and where is it?
And does everyone go there
or just some people?

And are they still aware of us?
Here on earth?
And if they are
can they communicate with us?
And we with them?

So many questions.
That need to be answered.
If your goal is to make peace.
With life.
With your life.

It's important to dance back-and-forth
until all the questions are answered.
No matter how long it takes.

Ask and answer.
Ask and answer.
Until the answers that find you
create peace.
For you.

This will not be easy.
Because there are so many forces that want to pull you back.
Here.
To be just like them.
They want you to go back to the way you were.
Before.

But you're different now.
Someone you love
dearly
has died.
And you've been cracked open.
Big time.

So you dance back and forth.
Between both worlds.

2. If You Are New To Grief

If you are new.
Brand new
to this thing called grief.
If someone you love
dearly
just
died
I would transport you to a beautiful room
with the most comfortable bed
you could ever imagine.
The lights would be low.
The music soft.
And you would control both by a simple thought.
"Dim the lights even more,"
or
"Raise the volume just a bit."

You would feel so safe in this room
that you would sleep
and sleep
and sleep.
Peacefully.
For as long as you wanted.
For as long as you needed.

As you began to adjust
spiritually
emotionally
mentally
and
physically
to this new life.

Your new life.

And when you were hungry.
There would be food.
Delicious
nourishing
extraordinary
food.
Prepared especially for you.
With love.
With great love.

And you could eat from your bed
food served on a tray
if that is what you wanted.

Or you could move to the chair.
That overstuffed comfortable chair
placed opposite your bed.

And you would decide if you wanted company in your room
or if you wanted to be alone
for now.
And no one's feelings would be hurt.
The world would know
that someone you love
dearly
has died.
And you have one job.
Just one.
To take the best care possible
of you.

I would transport you to a beautiful room
with the most comfortable bed
you could ever imagine.

And you would stay there as long as you wanted.
As long as you needed.

You would stay there until you felt ready
to take your next step.

3. *Hold On. Hold On. Hold On.*

In the beginning —
and I put no time limit
on the length of the "beginning" of your grief journey
because for some it may be weeks
for others it may be months
and for still others
the "beginning" may be years —
very often
the very best you can do is hold on.

I remember
the days
and weeks
and months after my daughter Erin died
when my mantra was
"Hold on.
Hold on.
Hold on."
Some days
some hours
some minutes
it was even hard for me to hold on to my
"Hold on" mantra.

I remember
the days
and weeks

and months after my wife Trici died
when my mantra remained
"Hold on."

And I remember
the days
and weeks
and months after my son Rory died
when all I could do was
"Hold on.
Hold on.
Hold on."

You are not alone.

If this is where you are
at the beginning of your own grief journey
and it takes all your energy
and then some
"just" to hold on
it's important to remember that you are not alone.

When it takes everything out of you
just to breathe.
When you wonder if another breath is even possible.
When you feel yourself slipping away into the darkness.
You are not alone.

There are many
many
many others
who have walked these same steps before you.

There are many others who have risen from the ashes.
You can too.

You can too.

But for now
hold on.
Hold on.
Hold on.

Have no expectations.
Someone you love
dearly
has died.
Your job is to breathe.
Just breathe.
Focus on that.

In the days after my wife Trici died
I was so shell-shocked
by the explosiveness of her sudden departure
that I told people my primary goal
each day
was to make sure I moved my eyelashes up and down
and up and down again.
That was the best I could do.
That was all I could do.

When your life has been shattered
in millions of pieces
you need to take it slow.

So be gentle
with yourself.
Be very
very
gentle.

Rest when you must.

I firmly believe that for many of us
if we were able to take in
really take in
the enormity of what has happened to us
we would not be able to live.
Literally.
I believe our bodies would shut down.
Our minds would turn off.
Our spirits would take flight.

Our new reality is simply too much to take in all at once.

So
we take it in
little-by-little
detail-by-detail.
Over time.
Lots of time.

And in time
(lots of it)
in small doses
our new reality begins to sink in.

Someone you love
dearly
has died.
Your life has changed.
Forever.
Many of your dreams have been shattered.

And for now
the best you can do is hold on.

Hold on.
Hold on.
Hold on.

Hold on.
Hold on.
Hold on.

You are not alone.

4. The Secret Is Out

The secret is out.

No more hiding.

In order to survive and kind of blend back in with everyone else
you pretend to be just fine much of the day.
Much of the week.
Much of the month.
Much of the year.

When you're at work.
(Can't cry there.
Can't bring my "problems" to work.)

When you are socializing with friends.
(People are tired of me complaining.
No one wants to hear about it anymore.
If I'm always a downer they'll stop inviting me.)

When you're with your family.
(Don't ruin Christmas/Easter/Mother's Day/Father's Day.
Can we have one family gathering when you don't cry?
We all miss him/her but can't you be happy for one day?
For me?)

You stuff your feelings.

You repress and deny any and every emotion that arises.

You try to look and act "normal"
hoping and praying
that one day you'll actually feel normal
again.

And people tell you how strong you are.
How "good" you are doing.
How great it is to have the old "you" back.

But you know a different truth.

You feel numb.
Empty.
Lethargic.
Hopeless.
Exhausted.

On the inside.

When you're really honest
and quiet
and alone
you know that you are a swirling cesspool of feelings and emotions
wanting to explode.

You're angry.
And you're not even sure what you're angry about.
Or who you're angry with.
God?
Them?

Him?
Her?
Life?
Yourself?

Deep down you're angry that life changed
and you don't know what to do about it.

You're sad.
Disappointed.
Frightened.
Overwhelmed.
Disgusted.
Lonely.
(Fill in the blank.)

You're wondering how
and if
you are ever going to be able to turn this ship around.

Recognize yourself in these words?
If so
take comfort in knowing that you are not alone.

What you are experiencing is common.
It's the old way of doing grief.
In fact it's the way most of us do grief.

And it doesn't work.
It causes pain on top of pain on top of unbearable pain.

Recognizing that this is the pattern you have fallen into
is the first step in changing your life.

And yes
you can turn this ship around.

There is a new way to do grief.

5. Choose Life

I can go back in the blink of an eye.
To the night of the day my 18-month-old daughter Erin died.
A hot sticky summer Wednesday.
July 18, 1990.

After everyone left.
My family.
A handful of friends who had heard the news.
After everyone left
it was Trici and I.
And an empty home.
An empty room.
An empty crib.

Two shattered people.
Lying on the wine-red Oriental rug
in the middle of our living room.
The rug that reminded me so much of my grandmother's house.
Holding Trici in my arms.
Crying.
Sobbing.
Weeping.
Wailing.

What will we do now?
What will we do now?
What will we do now?

Our daughter is dead.

And as the night grew darker
Trici got quieter
and I could tell by her breathing
that she had fallen asleep.
In my arms.
Finally.

And now it was me
and me
and the dark darkness.
Alone.

What will we do now?

And very clearly
and very methodically
I created a plan.

I would slowly
and gently
unwrap myself from my wife's body.
I'd walk into the kitchen

and grab the sharpest knife
from the wooden block we had received as a wedding gift.
And I would stab Trici
and then stab myself.

No note would be necessary.
Surely they would understand why I did what I did.

I could walk into the kitchen.

And as I lay there
on the red-wine Oriental rug
I played and replayed
that scenario
over
and over
and over
in my mind
as I listened to Trici's rhythmic softened breath.

What will we do now?

And after some time passed.
I have no idea how much.
I was startled to hear another voice
too.

So quiet
so soft and tentative
so fragile.

A whisper really.

A bold whisper
whispering
to me.
"Or you could live."

"Or you could choose to live."

I don't know how long I lay there
mulling over my two options.
Back and forth.
Back and forth.
Back and forth.

I don't know how long I lay there.

But the whisper grew louder
and stronger
and bolder
and life itself had other plans for me.
For us.

I decided to live.

I decided to choose to live.

It's a decision I've made
many
many
many times since.
In the face of my daughter's death.
In the face of my wife's death.
In the face of my son's death.

It's a decision you will have to make
too.

Not just once.

But over
and over
and over again.

Choose life.
Say yes.

Regardless of and in spite of.
Life has other plans for you
too.

6. The Unpredictability of Grief

If you are working with a
therapist
counselor
social worker
grief expert
minister
priest
or anyone else
who is trying to help you navigate the wilderness of grief
and they start talking about
the groundbreaking observations of Elizabeth Kubler-Ross
suggesting there is an orderly
predictable
unfolding of grief
please
please
please.
Do yourself a favor.
Leave.

People who are dying often
experience five stages of grief:
denial
anger
bargaining
depression
and acceptance.

They are grieving their impending death.
This is what Elizabeth Kubler Ross observed.

People who are learning to live with the death of a beloved
have a different process.
It isn't the same.
It isn't orderly.
It isn't predictable.

Grief is wild
and messy
and unpredictable
and uncertain
and ever-changing
and unsettling
and unnerving.

Everyone grieves.
Everyone.

Grief is the internal, automatic response to loss.

If you are alive and have attached to something.
Anything.
A job.
A pet.
Your health.
Your looks.
Your house.
A person.
A certain lifestyle.

Your car.
Anything.

If you have attached to something
and you lose that something
you grieve.
Automatic.
Internal.

And as much as I'd like to tell you that grief will be
orderly
neat and tidy
predictable
and unfold in five stages
it will not.
Period.

Most of us (all of us)
are ill-prepared
and ill-equipped
to go with the flow of grief
when it is our time
because
we never talk about it.

What it's like to live with grief.

Grief expresses itself
in surprising
and confusing ways.
There may be times when all you want to do is sleep
and other times when you can't sleep at all.

There may be times when you eat
and eat
and eat
and other times when you have no appetite.
You may feel
confused
sad
anxious
desperate
angry
frightened
lonely
nauseous
numb
dazed
dizzy
to name just a few of the ways that grief expresses itself
seemingly all at the same time.

And when your arms physically ache to hold your beloved
when you have heart palpitations
and stomach pains
and fight to keep your balance
this too is grief.

You think you are going crazy.
You are not.

You have entered the wilderness of grief.

And in order to get out
you must go through.
Period.

You must give yourself permission to mourn.

7. Choosing to Heal

In order to heal
you must mourn.

You must push grief
up and out.

Contrary to the old way of doing grief —
denying
suppressing
pretending
and stuffing your feelings and emotions down —
you must find ways to feel
express
honor
and release
all of the feelings and emotions that are bubbling up inside of you.

You must give yourself permission to mourn.

You must actively pursue your own healing.

Time alone will not
and does not
heal.
You've been lied to.
It's what you consciously decide
to do with your time

that matters.

That determines whether or not you will heal.

There is a new way to do grief.

First you must set the intention to heal.

You choose to heal.

And then you create a plan.

Concrete.

Measurable.

Doable.

Here are five things you can do to heal.

Starting today.

Pick one

just one

and commit to doing it every day for the next week.

1. Write in a journal.

Every day.

Write about what you are feeling

thinking

doing

hoping for

fearful of

or dreaming of.

Start somewhere and let it flow.

See what comes up and out.

Fill one page every day with written words.

No censoring.

Journaling is a concrete way to mourn.

2.   Spend 15-20 minutes a day in silence.
Just you
and you.
Listen.
To your breath
to your heart beating
to the birds singing.
Listen to God whispering
to you.
Listen for the voice of the one you love
dearly
who died.
Light a candle
savor a cup of tea
doodle
treat yourself to a warm bath
meditate.

Slow down.
Reconnect.
Spend time in silence
with you.
And listen.

3.   Commit to crying.
Say yes to crying.
Allow yourself to cry
every day
reminding yourself that when you cry
you heal.
Crying is the body's way of clearing out the old
and making room for the new.

Cry.
Cry.
Cry.
And when you do
say over
and over
and over
"I am healing
I am healing
I am healing."

4. Start a Gratitude Journal.
Look for things throughout the day
to be grateful for.
Write down three to five things every day
that you are thankful for.
Every day.
This practice alone
has the power to change your life.

5. Rebuild your broken body.
Walk outside every day.
Eat healthy.
Drink eight glasses of water a day.
Exercise.
Practice yoga.
Attend a Zumba class.
Get a massage.
Nourish your body.

6.   If there is something else you'd like to add to this list
that will help you heal
add it.
You know best what you need to do to heal.

We are mind and body and spirit.
Nothing is separate; all is connected.
Consciously work on one aspect of yourself
and you work on your whole self.
The goal is to add one thing
one thing
to your day for the next week
with the intention
the goal
the purpose of healing.

Begin exactly where you are.
Today.

Next week.
Repeat.
Over
and over
and over again.

Commit to your own healing.

8. I Thought She Was Lost

I thought she was lost.

Literally.

Having never really experienced the finality of a physical death before
for the life of me
I could not figure out what had happened.

Where was she?

The morning of July 18, 1990
my 18-month-old daughter Erin was diagnosed (finally)
with hemolytic uremic syndrome.
She'd spent the past four days
in and out of hospitals
and we were relieved to hear
the doctors say
finally
"We know what she has
we know how to treat her
she will recover."

She died that afternoon
at 5:10 pm.
It was a Wednesday.
I have a piece of paper to prove it.
And for the life of me I could not figure out what had happened.

How could the person I love most in life vanish?
Vanish.
As if a hand reached down and snatched her.
Snatched her.
From our arms.

I looked up at the stars
from the end of the pier
surrounded by water
and cried out
with my silent words
and my shattered heart
and my aching body
and my weary self
"Where are you
where are you
where are you?"

For the life of me I could not figure out where she had gone.

Where are you
where are you
where are you?

I asked
and I asked
and I asked
and I asked.
Over
and over
and over again.

And days passed
and weeks passed
and months passed
and a year or two
and maybe even three or four years passed.
To be honest I can't remember how long it took.

But I finally decided to believe that she had gone home.
In just 18 short months
my daughter Erin completed the work she came here to do.
(I thought that was remarkable.)
So she left her physical body
and returned to the source
to the beginning and the end
to all that is
was
and ever will be.
She returned home.
To love.
Itself.

And I realized that she had never been lost.
It was I who was lost.

But not so much anymore.

9. *Question Everything*

My 18-month-old daughter Erin died
from hemolytic uremic syndrome in 1990.

My 43-year-old wife Trici died
from a protein C deficiency in 1999.

My 13-year-old son Rory died
from brain cancer in 2005.

I have learned a thing or two about life
and death
and grief
and healing
over the past 20+ years.

I have learned that the death of someone we love
dearly
cracks us open.

It is supposed to.

It is essential that you understand that.

You will never
ever
be the person you were
before

the person you love
dearly
died.

Never.

Ever.

Until you surrender to that truth
you will not heal.

Until you release the energy you focus on trying to
yearning to
longing to
go back to the life you had
you will not have the energy you need to create your new life.

You will remain stuck in limbo.
Stuck between lives.
Some people stay there forever.
In that in-between stuck place.

The death of someone you love
dearly
gives you the opportunity to question everything.

Everything.

It is supposed to.

You are supposed to feel
like the very core of your foundation
has been shattered in a million pieces.

You are supposed to question every single belief
you held true and dear.

When you do this
you will discover that many (most)
of the beliefs you've chosen to hold on to
no longer serve you.

And you begin your search for new beliefs.
Beliefs that complement the new you that is emerging.

This can be exciting
challenging
frustrating
scary
invigorating
confusing
and hopeful all at the same time.

This is life.

Like a fragile tender seedling.
Which is you.
The new you.
The new you emerging.

Wiser.
More compassionate.
Stronger.
More vulnerable.
Flexible.

Some of the beliefs that you may have to question
release
and replace with new beliefs
may include:

1. If and when I pray hard enough
and in the right way
with the right words and mindset
God will do exactly what I ask him to do.

2. I cannot communicate with people I love after they die.
And they can't communicate with me.

3. The death of a person I love ends that relationship.

4. Feeling my feelings and emotions prevents me from healing.

5. I need to buck up and stay strong and keep busy.

You must question everything.

Each question asked
and each answer that arises
allows you to step into the new you that is emerging.

The you that you were born to be.

Question. Everything. Always.

10. Sit Down

I invite you to sit down.

In the chair next to me.

I will breathe with you.

In and out.
In and out.
In and out.

So your mind can slow down.
And your heartbeat can soften.
And your body can begin to release
the tension and tightness
you have been carrying for such a long
long
long time.

It is okay for you to speak.
Or to remain silent.
For as long as you like.
For as long as you need.

When you are ready to talk.

I will listen.
To all of it.

Start wherever you want.
At the beginning.
The middle.
The end.

It is okay if you jump around.
If you repeat yourself.
If you forget some of the details
or some of the order
and have to go back and start over.

It is okay with me if you cry.
A lot.

I'll give you the opportunity
to tell me about the death of your beloved.

All of it.

I'll let you tell me about the day your life changed.
Forever.

So many people ask me
"Is healing possible?
And if it is possible
what do I do?
To heal?"

Yes
healing is possible.

And contrary to popular belief
part of the way you heal is to tell your story
over
and over
and over again.

Why?

Because the truth is
that at the time of your loved one's death
if you were really able to fully grasp
the magnitude of what happened
and all its implications
you would most likely not be able to survive.
Literally.

If the breadth
and scope
and all-encompassing reach
of your beloved's death
came crashing down on you in one explosion
you
yourself
would implode.

It's just too much.

So
your spirit
your mind
your body protects you
by allowing the truth to sink in slowly

over time
at a pace you can live with.

And it's in telling the story of what happened
over
and over
and over again
that you are able to see and come to know the truth.
The magnitude.
Of what has happened.

It's important to comb through the details.
To relive the sights
the sounds
and the smells.
Go ahead and ask
"What if and Why didn't I and If only?"

Make sure nothing is off limits.
Look in every corner.
In every crevice.
Turn over every rock.

So that nothing is secret
or hidden.
So that no part of the experience is hands-off
or locked behind a closed door.
Allow no part of the experience
you've lived through
to have any kind of power over you.
Walk through all of it.

And yes
it's painful.
Especially at first.

But keep on telling your story.
Over
and over
and over again.

And after much time has passed.
And you've told your story
more times than you can possibly remember.
You will come to the day
when you begin telling it again.
Like you've done
so many hundreds of times before.
Because you know
that telling the story is a path to healing.

And you discover
that you can't tell it.
Not one more time.
You don't have the energy
or the desire
or the strength
or the need to tell it one more time.

You just can't do it.

And with your exhale
you say to yourself
"This is what healing feels like."

I invite you to sit down.
In the chair next to me.
And when you are ready to talk.
I'll listen.
To all of it.

11. I Am No Stronger Than You

I am no stronger than you.

I do not possess super-human-powers
that have somehow made me hurt less.
Than you
or anyone else.

Remember.
My 18-month-old daughter Erin died in 1990.
That explosion rocked my world to its very core.
Destroyed it.
And me.
And could have destroyed my marriage.
If I didn't hang on.
For dear sweet life.

And then my wife Trici died.
In 1999.
On New Year's Day.
The day before
what would have been our daughter Erin's 10th birthday.
Had she lived.
The unimaginable
unfathomable
impossible
became my reality.
My new life.

And yes
I considered suicide after Erin died.
And most certainly after Trici died.
I am no stronger than you.
I am human.
Like you.
And the death of someone we love
dearly
smashes us into a million little pieces.
And then some.

And when my 13-year-old son Rory was finally diagnosed.
After months and months of mistakes.
With terminal brain cancer.
Glioblastoma multiforme.
I lived in constant fear.
That he would die.

And I would live.

Fear balanced with hope that we could create a miracle.
If we "held the vision"
said the prayer
danced the dance
and chanted the chant.
I was told over
and over
and over
that I had the power to create my own reality.
I wanted my son to live.
I wanted to create that.

He died on February 22, 2005.
Anyway.

I am no stronger than you.
I am human.
Like you.

But I may be a bit wiser than you.
Now.
At this moment.
Because of the decisions I've made and the lessons I've learned.

So I can offer light.
And hope.
And possibility.

I did grief differently after Trici died.
And most certainly after Rory died.

I allowed myself to feel.
As many feelings and emotions as I could.

And some of the hundreds of feelings and emotions
that bubbled up in me were
fear
and anger
and sadness
and despair
and confusion
and loneliness
and hopelessness
and every other way that grief expresses itself.

Rejecting the old way of doing grief
I allowed myself to feel those feelings and emotions.

And in doing so
I was thrust into the deepest
darkest
blackest
seemingly endless pit of despair.
For a time.

Complete
utter
indescribable
despair.

Perhaps you have been there.
Perhaps you are there right now.

In that pit.

And
during that time
I realized that grief is not the enemy.

Grief is not the enemy.

Grief is the teacher.
The powerful
blessed
gift-from-God teacher.

But you must be brave enough to enter the pit.
By feeling your feelings.

You must be brave enough to recognize
acknowledge
and turn away from all of your soft addictions.
The activities you cling to in order to stay numb.

Numb to your feelings and emotions.
To life.
And to wisdom.

Soft-addictions
like watching endless television.
And shopping.
Nonstop.
And playing mindless electronic video games.
Over
and over
and over again.
And eating to fill the bottomless hole.
In your heart.
The hole that's there because someone you love died.
And drinking.
And drinking some more.
And relying on prescription meds
kidding yourself by saying they must be okay
because "The doctor knows I'm taking them."

I am no stronger than you.

In fact
I was engulfed in despair.

And because of the complete
and utter
despair
I found myself in
I decided to give myself permission to mourn.
To feel.
To enter the pit.

"There has got to be another way,"
I thought.
"I can not keep repressing
denying
pretending
and numbing.
I must do something different.
I must discover my next step."

And I did.

Discover my next step.
And I took it.
And then I took the next step.
And the next.

By feeling
honoring
and releasing
my feelings
I began to crawl out of the

deep
dark
pit.

And you can too.

I am no stronger than you.

12. Miracles

If you are like me
you have prayed for a miracle.

Or many.
Miracles.

Perhaps
like me
you've tried to use the power of prayer
to change the mind of God.
More than once.
That's what I thought a miracle was.
Saying the right prayer
at the right time
in the right way
with the right people
to get God to see things my way
and change the direction life was moving in.

I wanted God to do life "my way."

I would guess that you've wanted that too.

On July 18, 1990
as my 18-month-old daughter Erin lay strapped in an ICU crib at
Rush-Pres.-St. Luke's Medical Center on Chicago's west side
about to undergo dialysis

for her just diagnosed hemolytic uremic syndrome
I prayed
and I prayed hard
for a miraculous
complete
speedy recovery.
So life could get back to normal.
So we could be a family again.

My daughter was dead within a few hours.

On New Year's Eve 1998
as my 43-year-old wife Trici
lay in an ICU bed
at Oak Park Hospital in Oak Park, Illinois
hooked to a ventilator
I prayed that God would miraculously
and spontaneously heal her.
So we could get back home
and continue raising our two sons
3-year-old Sean and 7-year-old Rory.
So we could get back to living the life
we had worked so damned hard to create
following the death of our daughter Erin.

Within hours my wife was dead
on New Year's Day 1999.

And in the winter of 2005
as I flew my 13-year-old son Rory to Houston, Texas
to try an experimental
controversial

incredibly expensive treatment
for the brain cancer that had been diagnosed
just a few short weeks earlier
I prayed that we would be the exception.
I prayed that God would use us to show the power of prayer
to change outcomes.
I prayed that this most amazing boy
with the terminal brain cancer
and the dead older sister
and the dead mother
would recover.

My son died on February 22, 2005.

If you are like me
you have prayed for a miracle.

We each have our own story.

And we hold on to beliefs about our stories.
Beliefs that can cause us incredible pain.

Beliefs such as:

He was stolen from me.

She died too young.

We were robbed.

I should have been there.

I could have saved him.

Her death is my fault.

I am not a good mother.

I was not a good husband.

I will never be happy again.

There will always be a great big hole.

Perhaps you are holding on to some of these painful beliefs.
Or other
similar
painful beliefs.

Author Marianne Williamson defines a miracle as
"a shift in perception."

That simple.
That profound.

A shift in perception.

I have grown to love this definition of a miracle.

This definition of a miracle gives meaning to my prayer.

Not to change the perfect mind of God
but rather to change me
my perception

of life as it is unfolding
and as it has unfolded.

So the miracle for me
is questioning the beliefs
I hold on to
that cause me pain.

And I ask myself
is it true that:

He was stolen from me?

That she died too young?

That we were robbed?

That I should have been there?

That I could have saved him?

That her death is my fault?

That I am not a good mother?

That I was not a good husband?

That I will never be happy again?

That there will always be a great big hole?

Or is there another way of looking at life?
At my life?
At my beliefs
about my story?
A less painful way?
Can a miracle occur?
Can I shift my perception about what happened?

So
when you pray.
If you pray.
Consider praying for that.

For a miracle.
For a shift in perception.

But only if you want to make peace with life.
Your life.

And only if you want to learn how to live a full
joy-filled life
with the death of your beloved.

Pray for a miracle.
Pray for a shift in perception.
Yours.

13. Heaven

Do you believe in heaven?

Do you want
desperately
with all you are
to believe in this magical
mystical
forever place?

Perhaps you're not exactly sure what it is.
Or where it is.
Or what we'll do once we get there.

Most of us say we believe that heaven exists.

Do you believe that your beloved —
your spouse
your partner
your child
your parent
your sibling
your dear relative or friend —
is there
waiting for you?

Do you believe that when you die
there will be a grand reunion?

There will be.

And you don't have to wait until you die.

For that reunion.

You don't have to wait until you
yourself die
and "go to heaven"
until you are reunited.

With your beloved.

That reunion can happen today.

But it's up to you.
You hold the key.
You determine the time.

I imagine
that when you die
there may be a bit of confusion.
On your part.
At first.

It may take you a little time to realize what has happened.
You have left your physical body.

There may be a slight adjustment period.
When you re-acclimate.
Realign.
Reconfigure.

Like a fog lifting.

It may take you some time to realize that
yes
this is heaven.
This is the reunion you've been hoping for.

This is real.

The same thing happens when someone you love dies.

You think they are gone.
Vanished.
You think that there is no more relationship.

Only "in our memories and in our hearts."

But
the relationship continues.
Always.

The person you love
that died
is right here.

Waiting.
Wanting.
Ready.

Doing everything that he/she can do
to let you know that they are right here.

Still.

Beside you.
Above you.
Below you.
In front of you.
Behind you.

Yes
they are in that perfect song
you hear at the perfect time.
They are in the butterfly
that seems to appear out of nowhere.
The bird.
The coin.
The feather.
The flower.
The scent.
The uncanny "coincidence."
The "dream."

Yes
that is him.
That is her.

As in heaven
there may be a slight adjustment period
for you
here on earth.
Until the fog lifts.
And you realize that you are not alone.

Don't make that period last longer than it needs to last.

Say to yourself.
Over
and over
and over again.

That is him.
That is him

That is her.
That is her.

We are together.

Always.

14. Words Have Power

It's the language you use
to describe the death of your loved one
that tells the story.

The story of whether or not you will heal.

And your language is deeply rooted in your beliefs.

Your beliefs about death
grief
mourning
resurrection
and life itself.

If you are like me
you subconsciously
inhaled
your beliefs
at an early age
without realizing (really)
the power they have
to create your feelings
emotions
and experiences.

You cling to them.
Your beliefs.

You fight for them.
You defend them and own them.

"These beliefs are mine!"

You don't even realize
that your beliefs
can stop you
from healing.
After someone you love
dearly
has died.
You hold beliefs that create pain
on top of pain
on top of unbearable pain.

Beliefs such as:

His life was cut short.

She was taken too soon.

I've been robbed of so many wonderful years with him.

I'll never forgive myself.

I never got to say good-bye. How can I be at peace? I should have been there.

She shouldn't have suffered that way.

He is gone forever.

You begin to heal
when you identify a belief
that causes you pain.
This is the first step.

The second step
is asking yourself
if this belief is true.
Is it really true?
Can you be 100% certain that:

His life was cut short.
(What if he lived the perfect number of years and months and weeks
and days and minutes and seconds? The perfect number.)

She was taken too soon.
(Who took her? If there is a force powerful enough to take her then
why would that force take her too soon?)

I've been robbed of so many wonderful years with him.
(What if you were given the perfect amount of time to spend with
him?)

I'll never forgive myself.
(Why not?)

*I never got to say good-bye. How can I be at peace? I should have been
there.*
(Why can't you say good-bye and then hello right now? In the very
same breath?)

She shouldn't have suffered that way.
(Is she suffering now? From the place she is now can she even
remember the "suffering" as you call it?)

He is gone forever.
(Really? Forever?)

The third step
is having the courage
and the wisdom
and being open to the grace
that allows you to release the belief
that has been causing you so much pain.
The third step is understanding
that what you thought was true
is not.
The third step is not easy.

And the fourth step
is identifying
and holding on to a new belief.
A belief that brings you peace instead of pain.
Light instead of darkness.
Hope instead of despair.

Life instead of death.

It's the language you use
to describe the death of your loved one
that tells the story.

The story of whether or not you will heal
because your language
is so deeply rooted in your beliefs.

What story are you telling?

15. Keeping Busy

Many well-meaning friends and family members
and even others
who are a little farther down their own grief path than you
may be telling you to keep busy.

"The best thing for you right now
is to keep very
very
very
busy."

They tell you how important it is
to fill your days with "stuff" to do.

So
not knowing what else to do
(Really
how could you know?)
you take their advice
and you work very hard
to fill your days with work
and errands
and task
on top of task
on top of task.

Keeping Busy

They tell you
that by keeping busy
you can keep your mind off of "it."
"It"
of course
being the truth
that someone you love
dearly
has died
and the world as you knew it
shattered in a million or more little pieces.

You hear people say
"It's so great to see you out and about.
You're really doing well.
You are so very strong."

While deep inside
you know the toll
that faking it
to please others
is taking on you
physically
emotionally
mentally
and spiritually.

You wonder how long you can hang on.
The pain seems to actually be getting worse.
You feel pain
on top of pain
on top of unbearable pain.

75

And at night
when you finally drop into bed
exhausted from all the scurrying
and the running
and the pretending to be just fine
you begin to get a glimpse of your new life.

Just a glimpse.

You begin to feel your feelings.
They bubble up.
They have to.
You can only deny
and repress
and numb
and pretend for so long.

And very often
this encounter with your feelings
is frightening
and overwhelming
and confusing
and uncomfortable.

It feels messy and
out of control.
You have been lead to believe
that feeling your feelings is the problem.

Nothing could be farther from the truth.

Feeling your feelings
is the path to healing.

Realizing
and remembering
that you are not your feelings
is the path to healing.

You are not sadness.
You are not anger.
You are not despair.
You are not loneliness.
You are not confusion.
You are not regret.
You are not guilt.
You are none of that.
Or any of the other feelings or emotions
that are grief expressing itself through you.

Remind yourself that every feeling and every emotion has
a beginning
a middle
and an end.

Practice meeting each feeling and each emotion
that arises
with compassion
and tenderness
and gentle kindness.

Remember that you are not these feelings
and you are not these emotions.

They are energy currents running through your body
rooted in the beliefs you hold on to.

You are not your feelings.
You are not your emotions.

You are actually a spirit
that has come to earth
to have a human experience.
And when you are finished
you will return home.

And part of your work
here on Earth
is learning to live a full
joy-filled life
with the death of your beloved.

16. You Are Stronger Than You Think

You are stronger than you think.

You are stronger than you know.

You are stronger than you feel
right now.

And you are stronger than you believe
in this moment.

You have already walked through fire.

And you can do it again.
And again.
And again
if necessary.

And so can I.

I drove downtown to the County Clerk's office.
I was surprised and delighted that there was no line.
I walked right up to the counter
and was helped in less than 60 seconds.
No waiting.

I had already printed the request form at home
using my computer and printer.
I filled it out ahead of time
and read through it again
to make sure everything was in order.

And when the woman asked how she could help me
I handed her the form.

As if I were handing a prescription to the pharmacist.

Or a receipt at the dry cleaners.

Or the claim check at a lawn mower repair shop.

My action seemed that ordinary and routine.

Eight years after his death
I was requesting a copy
of my 13-year-old son Rory's Death Certificate.
His Death Certificate.

As I said
I have already walked through fire.
And so have you.
Many times

You are stronger than you think.
Know.
Feel.
Believe.

You have walked through fire.
And you can do it again.

Take a deep breath
and think about something you have done recently
that required extraordinary strength
courage
and even grace.

Something that most people don't do in a "normal day."
Something like me requesting a copy of my son's
Death Certificate.

Take a deep breath
and remind yourself
that you have already walked through fire.
Remind yourself that you are stronger than you know
than you think
than you feel.
You are even stronger than you believe.
Remind yourself that you can walk through fire again
if
and when
it is necessary.

When was the last time you walked through fire?

You are stronger than you think.

17. Signs and Symbols and Messages

We want the same thing.

If you are like me
you want to know
that the people you love
who have died
are safe.

That they are happy
and healthy
and whole again.

That they know
you ask for forgiveness
and that you forgive them.

You want to be sure that they know
how much you loved them
while they were with you
in their physical bodies
and how much you will continue to love them
now that they have returned to their spirit form.

You want their reassurance
that they know
you did everything you could
to keep them alive.
With you.

You want them to know
that they will not be forgotten.
And that your deepest hope
is that you will see them again
when it is your turn
to leave your physical body.

So you ask for signs.
You pray.
You plead.
You beg.
"Give me a sign that you are still here."

And you hear that favorite song on the radio
at the perfect time
in the perfect place.
And then you hear it again
and you wonder
could it be?

And you notice the butterfly
appearing when you need to see it most.

As if it knows the cry of your heart.
And you wonder
could it be?

And the bird taps at your window.
And comes back
again
and again
helping you feel a connection.
And again you wonder
could it be?

And you see their name on a billboard
and on a license plate
and in the newspaper.

And you see them in a dream.
You can feel them.
Hear them.
Hold them.
And you wonder
could it be?

And I say to you
over
and over
and over again
yes.

Yes.
Yes.
Yes.
This is your beloved talking to you.
He is telling you he is okay.
She is telling you that she is still here.

And you go to see the Long Island Medium
and she tells you the same thing.

And you read Sylvia Browne's books
and John Edwards' books
and James Van Praagh's books
and they all say the same thing.

They say yes.
Yes.
Yes.
It is your beloved.

And you visit a medium
in your own town
and you pay money
to ask the exact same questions.

Could it be?

And you seek confirmation from your pastor
or priest
or rabbi.

As I said
we all want the same thing.

We want to know
that the people we love
that have died
are okay.

Sooner or later
you will come to the place
where you realize a river is flowing.
And people are standing on both sides of that river.
People like you.
People like me.

On one side of the river
are the people who have made the conscious decision
(and it is most definitely a choice)
that yes
yes
yes
the signs
the symbols
the messages

the dreams

are all coming from the people we love who have died.

Our beloveds are using all their energy

all their power

all their creative resources

to let us know that they are okay

happy

healthy

whole

and home.

Surrounded by

and basking in

a love that knows no definition.

The nice thing about being on this side of the river

is that once you are here

you stay here forever.

Because you find peace

and contentment

and happiness

and joy

knowing what you know.

People are standing on the other side of that same river

who continue to wonder.

They continue to ask

"Could it be?"

Some of them notice.

The song.

The butterfly.
The bird.
And they ask
over
and over
and over
and over again
"Could it be?"
And others on that same side of the river don't even notice.
Their eyes are shut.
Their ears are tuned out.
Their hearts have closed.

There is also a bridge.
That will take you from this side of the river
to the other.

And all you need do is say yes.
Yes.
Yes.
Yes.
Today I make the conscious decision
to believe that we are still connected.
That I can communicate with you
my beloved.
And you can communicate with me.
Still.
That the signs

the symbols
the messages
the dreams
are all love notes from you.
To me.

And that one decision
the decision to say yes
will make all the difference.
For the rest of your life.
That one decision will help you heal.

Decide to say yes.
Choose to say yes.
Say yes.

18. Dying On Time

"His life was taken from him much too early,"
said the priest
about the 24-year-old soldier
who died while serving our country.

"His life was taken from him much too early."

It's a painful belief
that many of us breathe in.
Unexamined.
Unquestioned.

He died too early.
She died too soon.

As if any one of us
can point to someone
who died "right on time."

The death of someone you love
dearly
cracks you open.
Wide open.
It gives you the opportunity
to question
everything.

Or
you may remain asleep.
Until the next time.

Who
or what
gives life?

Who
or what
takes life?

Ultimately?

In the biggest picture?
The picture
that is so enormously big
that we can't begin to fathom it.
Yet
we try.
And I think we should.

Who
or what
gives
and takes
life?

Is this true all of the time?
Or just some of the time?

Who do you become
when you believe
that the person you love so dearly
was "taken from you much too early?"

Who do you become when you believe that?

And when you believe that
who does your version of God become?
And how do you feel about a God
who allows the people you dearly love
to die "much too early?"

And who would you be
and how would you feel
and how would you live life
if you decided to believe that God
whatever you believe God to be
only allows each of us
to die right on time?
Regardless of the circumstances of our death.

What if you decided to believe
that it could be no other way?
That everyone dies right on time.
Even if you don't understand it.
And never will.
While you're in your physical body.
Who would you be
if you decided to believe
that everyone dies at the perfect time?
Everyone.

19. Creating a Space for Hope

I remember that Thanksgiving of 1990.
Our first.
After the death
just four months earlier
of our 18-month-old daughter Erin.

Our hearts were broken.
Open.

Our life had been shattered.

I did not know how we would survive
or why we would even try.

The pain was so intense
there were times
I could hardly breathe.
I know you know that feeling.

My wife Trici and I
had made the conscious decision
to defy "conventional wisdom"
that suggests no big changes for that first year.

Instead
we followed our intuition
which reminded us over

and over
and over again
that we loved being a family.

So
early on
we set the intention
to have another child.

And it was that first Thanksgiving morning
the one four months after Erin's death
that Trici found out she was pregnant.
That "we were pregnant"
as she always said.

And
that morning
 at Old St. Pat's Thanksgiving Day Mass
as we turned to
our beloved daycare provider Marilyn and her son Aaron
to share our news
I felt a bit of hopeful joy
bubbling up from my core
mixed in with the sadness
and confusion
and anger
and despair
and bewilderment
and all the other feelings and emotions
that are expressions of grief.
I felt a bit of hopeful joy.

And I realized that
it doesn't have to be an either-or situation.

One feeling can sit right beside another feeling.

It doesn't have to be "all or nothing."

Make sure you set the intention
make the decision
to create a space for hope
for possibility
for peace
for relief
for gratitude
and yes
even for a bit of joy.

Make sure you keep that door open
even the tiniest bit.

It does not have to be "all or nothing."
One feeling can sit right beside another feeling.

You can create a space for hope.

20. Gifts Given and Received

I'm not sure how I would have responded
or what I would have thought
or felt
had someone suggested
that there were gifts
given
and to be received
following their deaths.

Not at first.

But now
when life has softened
and I have become more comfortable
in this skin
and with this life
I can say with such certainty
and gratitude
that
"Yes
there have been gifts given
and received."

When my daughter Erin died
I did not think I would survive.
There was no light.
None.

At the end of the long
dark tunnel
that twisted
and turned
and seemed to go nowhere.
There was nothing but darkness.

But
in time
and with a lot of hard work
I did discover
a gift.
Many gifts in fact.

My daughter Erin helped me feel whole.
For the first time.
When I held her in my arms.
When I stared into her eyes.
I felt whole
finding that piece
of me
I'd been missing
for many
many years.

And I was grateful.
That she had been born.
That she lived.
And that I was her daddy.
Always.

And I discovered that gratitude
opened the door to healing
and love
and life.
Again.

My wife Trici's death was such an explosively catastrophic
inexplicably paralyzing
out-of-body experience
that even though I knew I would survive
I wasn't sure I wanted to.
I had done it before.
I knew I could do it again.
I just wasn't sure I wanted to.
Along the way
I discovered
that this time
that long
dark
twisting-turning-to-nowhere tunnel
had a light at its end.
Calling me.
Pulling me towards it.
I wondered though
would there be gifts?
Again?
Could there be?
Could I find them?

And in time
with a lot of hard work

like before
I discovered there were.

Gifts.

She loved me.
Truly.
Deeply.
Completely.
As unconditionally as is humanly possible.
And after 13 years of marriage
I was finally able to grasp
that truth.
Trici loved me.
Simple.
Profound.
Life-changing.
She loved me.
And I loved her.

And I loved being a dad.
And in her physical absence
a mom.
I grew to
love
love
love parenting our two living children.
Rory and Sean.
I told them our lives would be different
following mommy's death.
But different was not bad

or less than.
Different was different.

And when Rory died
my fear was not for him.
Ever.
I knew he would be fine.
As his adventure continued.
My fear was for me.
I knew I would survive.
But was not sure I wanted to.
Not again.
Not again.
And I was surprised to discover
that the tunnel
the long
twisting
turning tunnel
was lit.
From the inside.
This time the tunnel was lit.
So I could observe
and participate.
And that made all the difference.

And the gift
one of them
that I discovered
was that I was capable of loving
my most amazing son
Rory
deeper

and louder
and stronger
with more fierceness
and tenderness
and understanding
and power
and gentleness
and completeness
than I had ever imagined possible.

I was able to love him big time.
And I did.
And that made me so proud.
And grateful.

I'm not sure how I would have responded
or what I would have thought
or felt
had someone suggested
that there were gifts given
and to be received
following their deaths.

But now
from the chair I sit in today
oh have there been gifts.
And I am so very
very
very
very grateful.

Search for the gifts.
They are there.
And when you are
willing
ready
and able
you will discover your gifts
too.

21. The Relationship Continues

What if I told you
that you will always have a relationship
with the people you love who have died?

Always.

And what if I told you
that those relationships
will either bring you peace
and comfort
and strength
and connection
and inspiration
or they will bring you pain
and loneliness
and heartache
and sorrow.

And what if I told you that the choice is yours?

You define the relationship.

You are either moving closer
to the people you love who have died.

Or you are pushing them away.
By building a wall.

When someone you love dies
it's your job to redefine the relationship.

It's your job to forgive
if forgiveness is necessary.

It's your job to say good-bye to their physical form
if that will bring you peace.
Just as it's your job to say hello to their spirit form
in the very next breath you take.

It's your job to ask for signs.
And messages.
To see with new eyes.
To hear with new ears.
To open your heart
and to know
without a shadow of a doubt
that yes
he is communicating with you.
That sign is from her.

Love is eternal.

The essence of who I am.
Of who you are.
Our soul.
Our spirit.
Our energy.
Is eternal.
There is no beginning.
There is no end.

You will always have a relationship with the people you love.
Even after they leave their physical body.
Even after they die.

You are defining those relationships right now.
Consciously or subconsciously.

Pay attention and define them consciously with love.
You will always have a relationship with the people you love.
Always.

22. The Horse

The truth is that most of us want to get back up on the horse.

That wild
unpredictable
breathtaking
heart-pounding
invigorating
horse called life.

Do you?

Even though you've been knocked off.
Knocked off the horse.
Even though you've been thrown off
and stepped on
and trampled
and bruised
and beaten
and broken by the fall
and now
you haven't a clue.

on.

That horse.
Your life.

But it's what you want to do.
It's what most of us want to do.

And to me
that is the miracle.
That is the shift in perception.

That wanting
that yearning
that desire for more
of life
is the miracle.

I believe
that it is life itself
whispering at first
"I am not done with you.
We have more to experience
more to explore
more to discover
more to create
more to enjoy
more to love
together

you and I.
Together."

Can you hear the whisper?
Ever so softly
at first.
Can you feel it?

After the fog begins to lift.
After the numbness starts to melt.
After the shock gives way to a deeper awareness.

In spite of the fact
because of the fact
that someone you love
oh so dearly
has died
you want to get back on the horse.
You want to live again.

You want to feel the warmth of the sun on your face again.

You want to smell the freshly cut grass in the morning.

You want to feel awe
again
when you look up at night and see the stars flung across the sky.

You want to feel like you belong here.
Among the living.
You want to feel safe
and connected.
You want to believe that there is a purpose to your life.
That you matter.
That you can contribute.
You want to love
and be loved.

And the truth is
you have two voices in your head.
And it feels like these two voices do battle every day.
One voice tells you that you will be okay.
That you will be happy again.
That life will feel good again.
That you can do this.
That you have the courage
the strength
the knowledge
the wisdom
the grace to live again.
Or for the first time.

And the other voice says "No."
It is too scary out there.
You will be hurt again.
You will not recover.

It is not possible.
The sorrow is too deep.
The loss too great.
You are doomed to a life of pain
of sadness
of suffering
of isolation
of desperation.

You get to decide which voice you listen to.

You get to decide which voice you make room for.
Which one you feed
and nourish
and pay attention to
and encourage to grow stronger
and louder
and more influential.

You get to decide which voice you say yes to.
Not just once.
But over
and over
and over again.

It begins with setting the intention.
The intention to say yes.

It begins with picturing yourself up there
on that horse.
Again.

Can you imagine that?
Can you see that?
Do you want that?

Can you feel what it would feel like
to be back up on that horse?

You were born to be radiant.
And so was I.

Not in spite of the fact that someone you love has died.
But because of the fact that someone you love has died.

Say yes.
Say yes.
Say yes.

Say yes to life.
Say yes to love.
Say yes to you.

ACKNOWLEDGEMENTS

As I wrote in the Introduction, this is the book I wish I had read after Erin and Trici and Rory died. But it hadn't been written yet. First I had to live it. Only then could I write it. For you. It's been a long, hard 20+ year process. There have been many, many starts and many, many stops. With my life. And with this book. There are many, many, many people to thank. Too many to list here. I trust you know who you are.

I do want to thank my parents for teaching me when my little brother Daniel Patrick died in 1963, when I was 6-years-old, that his death did not end our relationship. Danny remains a part of our family to this very day. We speak of him, remember his birthday, as well as the day he died, and always include him as number 5 in our family of 8 children.

Thank you to my friends Amy LeFebre and Paula Page Tierney for helping me edit this manuscript.

Thank you to my clients for your courage, your tenacity, your grace and your trust in me. For believing that yes, indeed, there is a new way to do grief.

Thank you to the thousands and thousands who are part of our Facebook Healing Circle. Every day you teach me about grief, and life, and love, and hope and possibility.

Thank you to each person who financially supported my campaign to create this book. Among those generous contributors are my friends Bob Ritchie, Shawn Reilley, Maureen Laughlin, Debra and Mark Whaley, Beth Paul-Peterson and Rita and Jimmy Farina.

I am honored to include these names among the pages of this book.

THANK YOU
R. Banford Exley
Virginia Garcia
Kristi Hayden
Mary Kay Morrison
Jasmine Patel
Laura Tomei

REMEMBERING YOUR BELOVED
Chase Anthony Apanian
Brock Alexander Barnard
Thomas Joseph Bechthold
Natalie (Tasha) Bueleson
Bethany Cadence
Jillian Alexis Crist
Landon James Hartner
Amanda Rae Hughes
Fred and Hazel Johnson
Chad Jones and Christa Jones Demo
Travis Lee Keathley
Jason Lammon
Joseph P. Kane, Jr.
Brilyn Carson Klubnik
Christina Faith Lewis
Blaine E. McDowell
James Christopher Ossenfort
Mary Margaret Petersen
Michael J. Prisco
Andre Reyna
Omar Javier Rodriguez
Craig V. Rudofski
Robert Sanford
Melanie R. Scoville

Paul Ian Sharples
Thomas L. Sterner, Jr.
Charlotte Elise Walker
Benjamin James Wasley
Teagan Lee Yoder

HONORING YOU AND YOURS

In Honor of Robert Alsot and Paul Kubski

Shannon Fisher honoring Jacob and Lukas Anderson

Penne & the Ard Family honor Mark Corbett Ard

Patte Armato Lund honors the memory of Joyce Armato

Roger & Beth Brackett honor The Alan Atwater Family

The Lathrop family remembers our beloved Cody Lyle Boardman

Berardino G. Bonaminio II - Amherst, Ohio - You are so loved!
Dad, Mom, Nick and Gina

Kimberly Brien Schneck remembers J. Patrick Brien

Debbie and Bev honor their fathers
Bud Chiodini and Jack Cicolello

Michelle Effron Miller in memory of my beloved son
Justin Taylor Creed

Susan S. Hurley honors her beloved husband Carl Joseph DeVoe

Margo DiBartelo honors Thad DiBartelo

Leisa Duncan honors Steve Duncan

Jane Edgell honors Jim Edgell

Sandy Greenstreet honors Jered Michael Goschie

Kim Bergeron remembers her son Austin Hawkey

Hendrik B. Helleman honors Vikki Helleman Kelley

In Honor of Erin Kathleen Jennings

Sara Ruble remembers Scott Michael Jessie

Connie Winch remembers her fiance Ron Knope: I loved you then, I love
you now, I will love you forever.

Frank and Marion Licari honor James N. Licari

Joan Brandt honors Dan Lundgren

Mary Zuba-Ingram thanks Ciss McInerney
for loving my brother Tom so well

Corey's mom honors Corey "Fire" Meyer

Sue Nova honors her beloved husband Dana Nova

Sandy Petersen honors Kevin Petersen

Carol Raymond honors Geoffrey Rau and Phillip Rau

Catherine honors Bob Rennert

Kathy Torrence honors Kent Ribordy and John Cordts Slack

Karen Schiller remembers Anna L. Schiller

Dan and Christina Smallwood honors
Payton Sweetness Smallwood

Amela Avdic honors her son Edo Spahic

Debra, Mclaren & Warren Spencer honor Jeff Spencer

Ellissa A. Schwartz lovingly honors Deloris E. Thoele

Cathy Wagner-Arntzen remembers Robert G Wagner

Dana Christensen honors Cameron Jon Weisz

ABOUT THE PAINTING

The painting on the cover of this book is mine. I am the artist.

I was born an artist. As a young child, art always brought me great joy. I have memories of begging and begging my older sister, Mary, to sit with me and color one more picture. "Just one more picture." She always did but frequently admonished me warning, "If you're not careful you'll turn into a crayon." I never did.

As I grew older, my grandfather, my dad's dad, was one of my biggest fans. He was my first (and to date) my only benefactor. When we would visit he always wanted to know where his masterpiece was. If I hadn't brought him one, he would get out the paper and crayons and ask me to create. With a huge smile, he would remind me to sign and date my piece, and then he'd hang it on the refrigerator. There was always an exchange of money involved, too. From an early age, my grandfather saw the artist in me.

In high school, I took every art class possible. I loved the freedom, the opportunity to socialize, the chance to create.

Of course, I majored in Art in college. And then got mad at a college professor my second semester freshman year and thought, "I'll show him." I changed my major to Special Education. And in doing so, abandoned the artist within me for many, many years.

But I married an artist.

And I expressed my creativity in other ways. Through music. Through the clothes I wore. Through gardening. By planning intricately detailed special events for many years.

But I abandoned the biggest piece of the artist within. The artist that created with paint, and color, and canvas and paper.

And then I moved to California after Trici died. With my sons Rory and Sean. My friend Jean told me about "Process Painting." Painting from the heart. Intuitively. Painting because of the process; not concerned with the product.

So, I tried it. I painted with Chris Zydel of Creative Juices Arts in Oakland, California. And I loved it. As I knew I would.

One of my paintings even let me know its name. "Revelation." Through that painting I discovered that I could move back to my hometown of Rockford, Illinois, a place I swore I would never return to. The painting let me know that after 20-some years, Rockford had changed. And I had changed. I could move back.

And I did. In August of 2002.

The house I purchased was contemporary. Lots of windows. Plenty of light. Trees. One side bordered a creek. A pool. Redwood exterior. It actually reminded me more of a house in Marin County, California than it did of a typical Rockford house.

It was different. Different from anything I had lived in before. New. A new beginning for me and my sons.

So, I set up my easel in the room with windows on three sides. Plenty of light. And I bought my canvas, my brushes and my paint.

And one afternoon I started to paint. Intuitively. I remember it so clearly because my son Rory stood behind me and just watched. The look on his face said it all. "I didn't know you had it in you, Dad."

And that afternoon, from a place deep inside of me, the painting birthed itself. While my son Rory watched in amazement.

It hangs over our fireplace.

And it graces the cover of this book.

I am the artist.

ABOUT THE AUTHOR

Tom Zuba is a life coach, author and speaker teaching a new way to do grief to people all over the world. Tom offers those living with the death of a loved one the tools, knowledge, and wisdom to create a full, joy-filled life.

Tom grew up in Rockford, Illinois with his seven brothers and sisters. When Tom was 6-years-old, his baby brother Daniel Patrick died suddenly of an undiagnosed heart defect. Danny's death was Tom's first experience with an intimate death. Tom graduated from Northern Illinois University in 1978 with a degree in Special Education. In 1985, Tom married Patricia Brennan in Oak Park, Illinois. Four years later, Tom and Trici welcomed their first child, a daughter, Erin Brennan Zuba.

On July 18, 1990, following a five-day illness, Tom's 18-month-old daughter Erin died suddenly from hemolytic uremic syndrome at Rush-Presbyterian-St. Luke's Medical Center in Chicago. Tom and Trici's son Rory was born one year later. In 1995, a second son, Sean was born.

On New Year's Day 1999, nine years after Erin's death, following a 52-hour hospital stay, Tom's wife Trici died suddenly at Oak Park Hospital in Oak Park, Illinois. A few days after her death, Tom learned that his wife died from a hereditary protein C deficiency. Tom's sons were 3 and 7.

Five years later, the night after his second day of 7th grade, Tom's 13-year-old son Rory had a seizure. The next two months were filled with doctor visits, medical tests, and hospital stays in both Rockford and Chicago where Rory's condition was misdiagnosed over and over again. In early November 2004, a biopsy which ended with the removal of Rory's left temporal lobe resulted in a diagnosis of glioblastoma multiforme, a terminal brain cancer. Deciding to forgo the customary chemotherapy and radiation, Tom and Rory travelled the country seeking alternative treatments. Rory died three months later on February 22, 2005 at OSF St. Anthony Medical Center in Rockford, Illinois.

Tom coaches clients one-on-one who are learning to live with the death of someone they love. He facilitates workshops and speaks at conferences and retreats throughout the country. He also works with social work, psychology, nursing, and medical students, as well as medical professionals, introducing them to a new way to do grief.

Shortly after his wife Trici died, Tom told his story on The Oprah Winfrey Show with best-selling author of *The Seat of the Soul*, Gary Zukav. Today, Tom and his son Sean are exploring life one day at a time in Rockford, Illinois.

To learn more please visit www.TomZuba.com. You can join Tom's Healing Circle at www.facebook.com/tomzuba1